THE RESEARCH WRITERS' PHRASE BOOK

A Guide to Proposal Writing and Research Phraseology

Susan Louise Peterson

D0899416

THE RESEARCH WRITERS' PHRASE BOOK

A Guide to Proposal Writing and Research Phraseology

Susan Louise Peterson

International Scholars Publications
San Francisco - London - Bethesda
1998

Copyright © 1998 by
Susan Louise Peterson

International Scholars Publications
4720 Boston Way
Lanham, Maryland 20706

12 Hid's Copse Rd.
Cumnor Hill, Oxford OX2 9JJ

Library of Congress Cataloging-in-Publication Data

Peterson, Susan Louise, 1960-
The research writers' phrase book : a guide to proposal writing and research
phraseology / Susan Louise Peterson.
p.   cm.

Includes bibliographical references and index.
1. Proposal writing in research—Handbooks, manuals, etc. 2. English language—Terms
and phrases—Handbooks, manuals, etc. 3. Research—Terminology—Handbooks,
manuals, etc. 4. Academic writing—Handbooks, manuals, etc. I. Title.
Q180.55.P7P48   1998   808'.066—dc21   98-5517 CIP

ISBN 1-57309-277-0 (cloth: alk. ppr.)
ISBN 1-57309-276-2 (pbk: alk. ppr.)

The paper used in this publication meets the minimum
requirements of American National Standard for Information
Sciences—Permanence of Paper for Printed Library Materials,
ANSI Z39.48—1984

THE RESEARCH WRITERS' PHRASE BOOK

Contains over 1,000 phrases
for writing research papers, articles,
grant proposals, thesis and doctoral dissertations.

Includes over 100 helpful computer research
phrases

Susan Louise Peterson, Ph.D.

For my parents who taught me that
the old ways were good

CONTENTS

FOREWORD

We are all familiar with the popular phrase, "A picture is worth a thousand words." Each of us in some way has experienced the reality of that phrase. The longer I stay in the field of education; however, I am even more convinced that a few words or phrases well-chosen are worth more than any picture can ever show us or teach us.

Most successful ideas that are really valuable and useful are simple and do not require volumes of discourse. Nor do they require an extensive exuberance of one's verbosity. *The Research Writers' Phrase Book* by Susan Louise Peterson can be described in three words—**simple, useful,** and **effective**. It is simple because it is straight-forward. It is useful because the phrases outlined in the book are categorical and are content specific. It is effective because it puts the reader in the driver's seat. You read what you need and apply it accordingly.

In this book, Peterson has captured in one volume a compilations of phrases that are common to research environments that can definitely help in the writing of a grant proposal, a position paper, a thesis or dissertation. Inertia is a common affliction if not disease of writing proposals of any kind. There is always the danger of "getting stuck." –and I might add a danger that becomes more high risk when time constraints are imposed and deadlines are fast approaching. Notwithstanding Murphy's Law, anything that can go wrong will, nor the KISS maxim, keep it simple stupid; there is a greater application of Flanner's Law with the successful use of this book. The more you work at something the luckier you are. *The Research Writers' Phrase Book* is a concise resource guide of tailored-made phrases that may be used as they are or adapted to the context of the material that is being discussed or presented. The more you work with the book, the luckier or more successful you will be. One caution—the book is not magic, but can save hours, if not days of painstaking writing time. The theme, "You can do it!" is the leitmotif of the book.

As the Dean of the School of Education at Fayetteville State University, a constituent institution of the University of North Carolina, I am always looking for resources that will assist with faculty development and refining the proficiencies of students, especially those at the masters and doctorate levels. *The Research Writers' Phrase Book* should be included in the "must read" category and I am confident that it will be used often.

Joseph Flanner Johnson, Dean of the School of Education
Fayetteville State University, A Constituent Institution of the University of North Carolina

PREFACE

Susan Peterson's *The Research Writers' Phrase Book* contains many valuable hints for individuals new to academia and useful ideas for those who need a fresh approach to their writing. Chapter One gives practical advice on how to get started writing a proposal and how to keep the momentum going during the process. Especially important is familiarity with the guidelines for the specific project. Susan's advice to new writers should help them clarify their objectives and direction and urges one to stay within appropriate guidelines.

The chapters that follow contain hundreds of relevant phases related to the most often used terms occurring in proposals, manuscripts and other documents. I feel that this guide could be especially useful to graduate students and others where English is not their first language. Sometimes it is difficult to get started writing a paragraph or sentence. With these phrases, you at least have a starting point. Often a sentence is obvious once you have a starting point.

I think the advice in this guide has the potential to improve clarity in writing, to reduce frustration and to save time. Clarity can be achieved through focusing on objectives as encouraged by Dr. Peterson. Choosing some of the suggested phrases provides variety that contributes to a more interesting final paper. I personally have on occasion spent considerable time at a keyboard trying to think of how to say what I know I want to say. Such a guide could have definitely reduced my level of frustration and saved valuable time.

Dr. Peterson makes a contribution to academic literature through her efforts in compiling the phrases and practical suggestions in this book.

Nancy Ferguson, Faculty-Clemson University Department of Crop and Soil Environmental Science

ACKNOWLEDGMENTS

A special thank you to my husband Alan, for his never ending patience of being married to a writer. His computer and typing skills are quite valuable to me since my typing and dexterity skills need much improvement. We have spent many late night hours at the computer until our eyes would water and heads would start to nod. I could not have asked for a more wonderful husband to share my life with each day and for this I am grateful.

I would like to think Dr. Robert West of International Scholars Publications for his wonderful support. He has been very helpful answering my multitude of questions and my early morning phone calls. I also appreciate his assistant, Anne and her help in faxing me needed information. I can not forget to thank Ginger McNally for her technical advice and willingness to help put the book in final form.

INTRODUCTION

This book is written for research writers who need help in coming up with phrases to compose proposals and research oriented writings. Many of these phrases are common knowledge in research circles and have been passed around for years. However, when a researcher is asked to write an article under a tight deadline, he or she may need a quick reference guide with common research phrases to pull the paper together. Depending on the purpose of the research writing, these phrases can be adapted and modified. They provide a framework to get the research writer thinking about the common word usage that is used in research areas. The book also includes some computer research phrases that would help the writer.

Many of these research phrases would benefit students writing term papers, as well as those working on graduate thesis and dissertations. Research professionals can find these phrases helpful for professional paper presentations, articles and grant proposals. This quick collection of research phrases can benefit beginners as well as establish research writers.

During my undergraduate and graduate years of college, I spent endless hours in the library. I read research journals until I was blue in the face and wondered if someday I might actually get a job in the library. Instead, I became a professor and teacher and I never lost the use for the library or books. The problem soon became time - How was I going to develop proposals for educational funding in a fast and concise way? I noticed that there was not really a good reference book with research phrases that would help proposal writers. I wish this book would have been around back in 1982, to help me on those late nights as I was composing my proposal for my doctoral dissertation. This book is a proposal writer's guide with over 1,000 research phrases and it even contains computer research phrases for up-to-date proposals. This book is the ultimate guide for proposal writers.

In 1982, I entered my doctoral program not having a clue about what proposal and research writing entailed. I was a twenty-one year old doctoral student who wanted to teach college some day. Developing a research proposal and learning to write in an acceptable academic style was challenging for me in my limited writing background. It all came together and I survived getting my Ph.D. at the tender age of twenty-three. A few patient professors took the time to give me the constructive criticism I needed (and still need), and encouraged me to come up with new ideas and phrases.

Since that time, I have really enjoyed reading and helping college students re-think and re-phrase their papers. I, like my students still get writer's block now and then when I'm composing a research proposal or paper presentation. I wrote this book to help others and myself stay focused on research topics by incorporating research phrases into our creative thought process.

CHAPTER ONE
INTRODUCTION TO PROPOSAL WRITING

What Is A Proposal?

A proposal, in its easiest form is simply a plan put forth by the writer to explain what he or she is going to do or accomplish. The proposal is often submitted to either an editor, advisor or department chair and later is usually considered for approval by some type of committee. There are different purposes for writing proposals. In the educational institutions, graduate students are developing proposals to describe their research plans and carry out the requirements for writing theses and doctoral dissertations. Faculty members, researchers and others in the academic world are writing proposals to get funding for grants to conduct community and research projects. Authors are also developing proposals to introduce editors to the books they are writing and the articles that are forthcoming. Whatever the purpose, a well-developed proposal that is organized and well thought out will more likely be approved than a weak, poorly organized plan.

Advice For Graduate Students Writing Proposals

Many times graduate students go into an initial state of shock when they hear other students talk about developing a research proposal to complete their Master's thesis or doctoral dissertation. Their undergraduate experiences often included writing term papers and book reviews, but nothing as extensive as a major research proposal. Panic often sets in and before long the graduate student is totally confused about the whole proposal concept. Some students will give up on this process, but others will start asking questions and seeking help from their advisors. I was lucky, I had a very positive experience writing my proposal and completing my doctoral dissertation. I want to share a few helpful hints that made this process easier for me and hopefully this advice will help you during your graduate studies.

1. Become Theme Oriented

People often ask me how I finished all my dissertation in two years. Basically, I had a theme in mind or an idea floating around at the top of my head. Some graduate professors gave us the freedom to write research and term papers on any topic we wanted to explore. I was planning to write my dissertation on the topic of fear of success, so with each term paper assignment I would write an aspect of fear of success. Basically, I was working on my literature review for my proposal of the doctoral dissertation, as I was writing research papers for my graduate classes. It also worked out well because my professors were giving me comments and feedback on my writing style. You are accomplishing two goals at once, by writing research papers on the same topic as you are going to be developing in your research proposal. Keep in mind that the theme or topic may have to be narrowed or refined to focus in on the specific purpose of the study or proposal.

2. Set A Time Frame

Graduate students often ask how long it takes to write a proposal, conduct research and finish the dissertation process. Some people finish in two years and for others it seems to take ten years. Check with the university you are attending because they usually have some kind of time limit to finish a dissertation. Work with your professors as much as you can while you are on campus to make this process easier and more convenient. Begin writing your proposal immediately. Some graduate students have the idea that they will complete all of the course work first, before even thinking about writing their proposals.

The problem with this thinking is that many graduate students have professional jobs and get transferred around the country. After they complete their course work, they may be relocated to a remote place with limited academic support. As a result, many graduate students spend hundreds of extra dollars on phone calls and trips back to the university to accomplish things that could have been done easily while they were on campus.

3. Pick Your Committee Carefully

Take time to pick your academic committee carefully. This is the committee that will be evaluating your research proposal and approving or rejecting your doctoral dissertation. Another consideration is to find faculty who work cooperatively with each other and the chair of the committee. It is helpful to find faculty that are truly interested in your subject area and are willing to work with you cooperatively during this long and sometimes stressful process. Listen to your professors as they lecture to you on topics that spark your interest. Do not hesitate to go talk with them about an idea you have for the proposal. They are usually good about giving you additional themes and suggestions, before you make your final decisions on what to write about in your proposals. In most cases, it is essential to pick at least one faculty member with an expertise in statistics. A good statistician can save you hours of time answering questions that other faculty are not equipped to answer. I suggest you get to know your research committee well, long before your proposal comes to the committee meeting.

4. Learn The University Writing Format

Before you even start writing your research proposal, make a trip to the campus bookstore or the graduate college and ask if there is a thesis writing manual with the university guidelines for proposal development. Some universities have developed specific graduate college writing formats and regulations. They require that all thesis, dissertations, and abstracts be done in a specific format and your proposal must be in compliance with this format. Some universities even require a signed statement from your dissertation advisor stating the reason you are deviating from the university format. If students are sloppy about the university writing format, they may end up rewriting and editing the whole proposal several times and no one wants to do that.

Advice For Faculty And Professionals On Writing Proposals

Faculty members and professionals, who attended graduate school survived the beginning process of writing a proposal and developing the idea into a full blown thesis or dissertation. Years later, they will often find themselves developing a grant proposal or request for funding again as a job requirement. Many of these college graduates have a good sense of writing, but they face stiff competition as more professionals are submitting proposals to be evaluated for funding. I have attended many grant writing workshops and several themes seem to be popping up at most of the workshops. The following are some hints to assist faculty and professionals who are writing proposals:

1. Write A Realistic Proposal

I know this sounds fairly basic, but sometimes proposals make claims or propose ideas that could never be carried out or completed realistically. Proposals must be realistic in their approach and time constraints. A faculty member with a 25% research appointment, who teaches classes the other 75% of the time does not really have that much time to conduct research. For example, writing a grant proposal with a large sample of single parents on the Mississippi Delta, that must be interviewed during a short semester, is likely to sound totally unrealistic to the reviewers evaluating the grant proposal. The reviewers know that the researchers would also have to travel to an area that they may be unfamiliar with to conduct the research. The proposal may be rejected on the basis that it is unrealistic and to difficult for the faculty member to complete the research study.

2. Writing A Proposal With A Team

You may have enjoyed your graduate proposal writing experience because you did the writing yourself and submitted it to your advisor and committee. Some professional organizations write grant proposals as a team. Basically, each person on the team is responsible for writing a part of the grant or research proposal and the team meets weekly or frequently to discuss the progress of the proposal. It is important for everyone to do their part and complete their writing sections in a timely manner. There are usually a few adults on any team that do not live up to their part of the proposal task and that hampers the rest of the team's work. A helpful suggestion is to have someone in a supervisor or leadership type role to get after those few team members who may fail to meet the deadlines and hinder the process of the proposal.

3. Don't Get Too Emotional About The Proposal

Most faculty and professionals take pride in their work and ability to write a proposal they are proud of presenting to others. However, when it is a person's job position to write a proposal, he or she must not get too emotionally attached to the ideas that are in the proposal. I experienced this first hand as a young faculty member, who was very idealistic and thought that by writing a grant proposal I would conduct the research the way I wanted to in the proposal. However, my department chair was the research director and she changed the proposal to suit her goals. Later, I had to circulate the proposal to an array of deans and administrators and they each made changes and edited the proposal. By the time the grant proposal was in the final draft, it was not even my idea anymore and had been shifted from my original goals. I learned quickly that when I was in a job position to write for others that I could not get too emotionally attached to the proposal.

4. Watch Out For Tight Deadlines

I wish I could say that faculty members had months and years to develop elaborate proposals, but unfortunately the world does not work quite that way. Many times a request for funding or grant proposal announcement guideline is routed through the university system. Hopefully, electronic mail and fax machines are improving this situation. However, the request may set on the dean's desk for several weeks and then go the department chair's office where it sits for a few more days. Finally, the department chair comes to you the overworked faculty member and wants an extensive grant in three days. You burn the midnight oil, pull the grant together and at the last minute (the day before the grant deadline) you get the final signatures. You then rush to the university office and express mail a huge box of the copies of the proposal, praying it meets the deadline.

I had what I call the proposal writers worse nightmare. I had worked all day and night writing a proposal and obtaining signatures at the last minute. I ran to the central university mailing office and had the package mailed with a guarantee of next day delivery with an express mail company. Little did I know that the university was trying to save money and they used a company that guaranteed next day delivery, but did not specify what time the package would be delivered. Another express mail company would have delivered the proposal by ten o'clock the following morning, but the university did not use that company because it was too expensive. To make a long story short, my proposal needed to arrive the following day by two o'clock. Instead, the proposal arrived at five o'clock and I received a phone call that the proposal was not accepted or even considered because it did not arrive before the deadline time. I was devastated because I had worked so hard on the grant and it was not even considered. My advice for the future is to watch those tight deadlines and find out the delivery times for the package. Since that time, I have talked to faculty members who have even paid the express mailing out of their own pockets to use a reliable company that guarantees the proposal will be delivered on time to meet the deadline.

Advice For Writers Developing Book Proposals

Writers should contact the academic publishers and request the guidelines for proposal submissions. Each publisher may have unique guidelines, but there will be some overlapping in the materials they request from the writer. The following is a list of some items that might be requested for an academic book proposal:

*Estimated length of book

*Time period for book completion

*Comparison of your book with other books in field

*Author's credentials and/or resume

*List of book & article publications by writer

*Target audience for the book

The following are some ideas and advice to help academic writers in developing book proposals:

1. Manuscript Completion

Some academic writers spend years on a book thinking it should be totally completed before they can submit it to a publisher. If a book interests publishers and they really like the sample chapters and proposal, the writer could get offered a contract prior to the completion of the book. On the other hand, if the book manuscript is completed some publishers would like to read it along with the proposal, especially for new writers. The writer can also make a calendar or timeline to focus in on the completion date.

I have friends who work on one book for years and never feel it is perfect enough to mail to publishers. Editors still may change their brilliant ideas no matter how many years the writer spends on the manuscript. Beware of some of those edit or script doctors who want to charge large amounts of money to edit your manuscript so that it will have more potential in the writing market. These people will make money off of you and there is no guarantee that the book will be published.

2. Get Publishing Directives

To save time and money it is important to know the publishing directive of the academic press. A query letter with a brief description of the book or a phone call (please note some editors refuse to take calls) can help you see if the press is even publishing books on your topic. I get letters from publishers stating they have their publishing needs met for the next two years and are not considering new material. I also talked to a publisher that had only published one book and she was still trying to figure out how to publish and distribute that one book. I knew not to waste my time and money mailing a book proposal to a company that was not established. Sometimes a simple query letter stating your ideas and the market audience for the book will allow the editor to make a decision. The editor will decide if the book is in the publishing direction of the press or if the writer should go elsewhere with the book proposal.

3. Controversy

An agent once told me that the big publishers like books with controversy. Publishers do not usually want to read a book that is just a summary of the same old material they have read a thousand times. A little controversy, a new angle or twist to an age old problem may be just the trick to capture the editors attention. Sometimes an unusual idea may catch the editor's eye and open up a new debate of an old topic.

4. Be Patient

It is hard for writers who are striving eagerly to get published to be patient. The new writers sometime have a preconceived notion that the editor is only working on their manuscript proposal. Response time is usually longer than expected and new writers get very anxious or impatient. The best advice I can give is to be patient and wait it out. The last thing writers needs to do is call up an editor and complain about the length of time they are taking on the proposal. Be patient! Editors are sometimes busy with other things such as editorial meetings, bookfairs, and book promotions. It takes them time to read a number of manuscript submissions.

HELPFUL HINTS FOR WRITING A BETTER PROPOSAL

There are so many little things that graduate students, faculty members and other professionals can do to write better proposals. Sometimes a small change can make a big difference in how the proposal is reviewed and evaluated. The suggestions for writing better proposals include:

1. A Catchy Title

Long, drawn out titles that sound plain and redundant do not catch the attention of reviewers that evaluate hundreds of proposals. Take a little time toward the end of the proposal development to brainstorm a creative title that reflects the meaning and make up of the proposal. A clear and brief title that gets to the point of the proposal is far more catchy than a long, redundant title that gives the reviewers an eye strain.

2. Follow The Proposal Guidelines

A proposal reviewer has criteria for judging the worthiness of a proposal. These criteria are often developed from the requested information of the applications. If you do not follow the proposal guidelines, it will be obvious to the reviewers. Some proposal guidelines require two proposals such as a technical proposal (telling about the project), and a business proposal (with budget information). There are mini-proposals for small projects as well as large competitive grant proposals. They all have guidelines and the writer should read and follow the proposal guidelines carefully.

3. A Relevant Problem And Purpose

The key word for proposals is 'relevant.' If the problem and purpose of your research proposal is not relevant and important then there is no good reason for even writing the proposal. Reviewers are usually eyeing clearly stated problems that are significant and have purpose. It may be necessary to define the problem and to make sure the reviewer understands the terminology and specific language used in an academic field that is in the proposal. This is your chance to sell the relevance of the whole proposal and the benefits of the study. If the problem is not justified and worthwhile to society, the reviewer may disregard the need for the rest of your proposal.

4. Include Objectives In The Proposal

I made the assumption that everyone pretty much understood what objectives were and that they needed no explanation. However, several seniors in college one day told me they had no idea what an objective meant and no idea how to write one. I found that really hard to believe, so I tried to simplify it. An objective is simply the aim of the study and should state what you want to accomplish in the proposal. Some people call the objectives the end results you are aiming for in the proposal. These objectives need to be in focus with the research goals of the university and funding organization.

5. A Thorough Literature Review

In our computer society an extensive literature review should be done for a proposal. The proposal writers should check to make sure that the research study has not been done before and to make sure they are on the right track. The literature review can be organized with sub headings to review various aspects of the proposed problem. Sometimes a historical literature review and a literature review of current research can be combined to provide a broad picture of the topic.

6. Appropriate Sample And Research Design

Reviewers unfamiliar with your proposal should be able to figure out your research design and sampling techniques without too much trouble. If you are unsure of what you are doing, find someone in a university statistics department to help answer your questions and give you sound advice. It is also important to discuss how the data will be analyzed in the study. A statistics consultant can offer helpful advice and quick direction in developing the research design, sampling and testing procedures.

7. Expected Results And Potential Of The Study

This is a good time to explain what you feel will be some of the long-term results of the proposed study. You can discuss the potential of the study and the influence and impact it will have on society. Do not miss this opportunity as another key selling point to convey the relevance of the study and why there is a great need to fund it. This needs to be a strong part of the proposal because if you don't expect much to come from the study maybe its not worthy to fund.

8. Extra Items

Many times a grant proposal will request extra items such as a resume or copies of previous publications. Whatever information is requested, make sure it is up-to-date and projects the best image of your professional abilities. The reviewer may be looking at your professional expertise to see if you are qualified to carry out the research project. For example, if the researcher is conducting educational research in public school classroom, there may be teacher certification requirements in the study. The reviewers could also be examining the amount of research time that is being devoted to the study, as well as budget and administrative issues.

9. Review The Proposal For Weaknesses

A good idea, if you have time is to read and review the proposal thoroughly to find weaknesses. Perhaps the problem was unclear or the literature review did not address certain issues. The writer can go back and rewrite or phrase items to make a more worthy and strong proposal. Ask a colleague to review the proposal and give you some feedback on weak and confusing areas. Sometimes just a brief change or omitting a few sentences can strengthen the proposal.

10. Don't Ramble

As I pulled out my yellow paged doctoral dissertation from the bottom drawer of the filing cabinet, I realized I had made some mistakes as I reviewed it thirteen years later. The major area that I would write differently is the literature review for my doctoral dissertation proposal. I noticed that there were certain areas that I had rambled off and left my central point of focus. I had some very well documented and worthy quotes, but some of them did not really apply to my topic. There were studies that I should have justified and explained how they were important to my research project. Basically, my advice is to stick to the topic and relate the literature review directly to the proposed research. It is very easy to wander off on a tangent that changes the focus and direction of your research proposal.

11. Pick A Topic You Enjoy

I know this sounds self-explanatory, but you are going to spend many hours writing and developing a proposal so it is essential that you pick a topic you really enjoy. Take some time and explore topics of interest on the Internet or in the library and see what sparks your interest. Talk with professors and colleagues about the topic you are considering for the proposal. They will often be good sounding boards and provide feedback for your proposal ideas. Be flexible to change your topic if it seems 'over-researched' or already studied. The more you enjoy a topic, the more excited you will become about finding new information and expanding your proposal. Those late night hours won't seem so long if you pick an enjoyable topic.

The following chapters contain research and computer phrases that will help proposal and research writers. Keep in mind that the phrases can be modified, adapted and changed to fit the particulars of your proposal and research. Best wishes on your journey to write a successful proposal!

CHAPTER TWO
PURPOSE
FOCUS
OBJECTIVE
ASSUMPTION
HYPOTHESIS

PURPOSE

the intended purpose of the report was

for the purpose of this paper

the purpose of the study was to determine

the purpose of the article was to contribute

from the stated purpose, research questions were developed

the purpose of this study was to explore

the purpose of this paper is to review

the primary purpose of the thesis is

the stated purpose of the study is

the purpose of the article is to critique

the purpose of the research is to assess

it is the purpose of this article to re-examine

a major purpose of this study is to explore

the purpose of this article is twofold

the purpose of the writing is to highlight

the purpose of the paper is to report

the purpose of the article is to alert others

the purpose of the pilot study was to

the author's stated purpose was

the purpose of the article was to compare

the purpose of the thesis was to evaluate

the purpose of the study was to re-evaluate

the major purpose of the investigation

the purpose of the paper is to illustrate

the purpose of the article is to discuss

the purpose of the dissertation is to analyze

the purpose of the dissertation is to take a historical look

the purpose of the dissertation is to explore the impact of

the dissertation was designed for the purpose

the major purpose of the dissertation is to provide an overview

the purpose of the dissertation presentation

the report's purpose was to

the author's purpose was unclear

in reviewing the article it was difficult to understand the purpose

the purpose of the study was to inform the readers

the purpose of the article was to develop a plan for

the grant's purpose was to establish

the purpose of this report was to outline

the purpose of the thesis was to develop a system to

the purpose was not accomplished in the study

the purpose was to broad to determine

the purpose was not achieved in the grant

the research article did not state a purpose

the term paper's main purpose was to

the purpose of the research was unique

the grant did not fulfill its' purpose

the purpose of the paper is to notify

the specific purpose of the term paper is

the purpose of this research is to compliment

the purpose of the study is to acknowledge

the purpose in the report was to advocate

the researcher's purpose was to affirm

the purpose of the article was to gain appreciation for

the purpose stated in the report was to assemble

the purpose and backbone of the research was to

the purpose of the study was to look at opposing viewpoints

the purpose of the research was to expand

the purpose was briefly stated

the concise purpose of the study was to

the purpose in the report had two essential points

the purpose of the dissertation was to make a chronological list

the collective purpose of the report was to

the purpose of this commentary is

the common purpose of the report was to

the purpose of this presentation is to compose

the purpose of the article was to confirm

the purpose coincides with previous research

the purpose of the grant is to address complex issues

the purpose of the term paper is to define

the purpose of the report is to plan a schedule of events for

the purpose in the article was to establish a directory for

the purpose was displayed for the participants to view

the purpose was to disseminate the information to

the purpose of the grant was to divide

the purpose of the project was to diversify

the purpose was to earmark

the editorial purpose was

the intended purpose was to

the author did not state the purpose

the purpose of the study was to broad

the purpose was difficult to comprehend

no specific purpose was stated

FOCUS

while the focus of this study is

specifically, this article will focus on

this paper attempts to focus

it will also focus on

the proposed research project will focus

the research article will focus on exploring how

the main focus of the article centers on

the thesis of my presentation will focus

the central thesis of this paper is to provide a focus

the article will focus on the idea of

the primary focus of the dissertation is

the research focus is

the focus of the article is to examine

the paper's focus is

the article continues to focus on

the focus of the writing is to explore

the term paper's focus is to equip the reader for

the focus was confusing

the focus of the exhibit centered on

the grant's focus was to formalize

the general focus of the project

the historical focus in the research was to

the focus of the dissertation was to research the influences of

the focus of the research will impact

the focus in the paper was to insure

the focus was not clearly stated

the focus of the study lacked direction

the focus was listed at the beginning of the paper

the focus was misconstrued by the research participants

the national focus of the grant is to

the focus was somewhat vague

the article focus was unconventional

the focus outlined on the paper is to

the focus of the study was extended

the research panel chose the focus

the focus was parallel to

the focus of the paper was paramount to

the focus was periodically revised

the pilot study focused on

the focus of the plan took a turn

the focus pointed toward

the study had a practical focus

the focus was established to

the focus was to recant an error

the researcher focus was to recount

the relative focus consists of

the focus surrounds the idea of

the specific focus included

the research focus was a spin-off of

the focus was structured around

the focus was subjective in nature

the research team focused the project on

the team worked together on a research focus

the traditional focus of the program

the paper has a nontraditional focus

the focus of the report was difficult to convey

the ultimate focus is

the focus was to demonstrate

the focus consisted of validating information for

the focus was to verify

the focus was coordinated with the research vision

the research focus was vital to the study

the focus is justified in the research

the focus of the research paper was well-done

OBJECTIVE

the objectives of the research were to

the primary objectives of this study were

the paper's objective can be viewed as

in writing the report, the objectives are

the objective of this study was to assess

the objective of the thesis is

the article's objective is

the author's primary objective is

the stated objective of the study is

the report's central objective

accordingly, the objective is

consequently, the objective of the paper is

the objectives were difficult to understand

the objectives attempted to

the author's objective was clearly stated

refer to the earlier objective

the basic objective in the term paper

the objective belonged in

beyond the objectives

the objective asserted that

the objective was broadened to include

the objective capitalized on

the clear cut objective

a close examination of the objective revealed

there was some concern about the objectives

the objectives concentrated on

the objectives were identified

the objectives confirmed

the research objectives contributed to the study of

the objectives were coordinated with

there was a correlation between the objectives

the objectives give credit to

the researcher's objective was critical of

the objectives seemed dated

the objective was developed promptly

there was a decision about the objective

the objectives demand

the objective clearly demonstrated

the dichotomy of the objectives

the objective was differentiated

it was difficult to comprehend the objective

the objective's direction was

it was discovered that the objective was

the disadvantage of the objective was

the dominant objective was

the objective was editorialized

the principle element described in the objective

the experimental objective was

the extensive objectives

the objectives fabricate

the finalized objective

the research forum's objectives

the historical objective was

the objective illustrated

the research objective was influenced by

the initial objective

the objective limited the

the above-mentioned objective

it was a notable objective

the precise objective

the proposed objectives in the paper

the objective was regarded as

the relative importance of the objective

the objective was revitalized

the root of the objective concerned

the schematic objective

the scope of the objective was to

the simultaneous objective appeared to be

the objective was a solid part of the study

the straight forward objective was

the objective was to survey

the typical objective would be

the objectives were to verify

one could view the objective as

the objective was visualized by

there was a weak objective in the study

the objective was characterized by

the objective can be compared to

contrary to the objective

the objective was to evaluate

ASSUMPTION

the assumption can be made that

the following assumptions are pertinent to the study

it is a common assumption

an important theoretical assumption

although, the general assumption is

the academic assumption

the assumption was put forth

the assumption was advanced by

the researcher's assumption was

all these assumptions surround

the assumption of the study seemed obvious

the assumption was articulated

the assumption applied to

the appropriate assumption would be

the article's assumption

the research team had assumptions about

the report listed the assumptions

assumptions were made about the research

assumptions were addressed in the study

the foundation of the assumption was

the paper focused on a theoretical assumption

general assumptions were made in the paper

common assumptions were directed at

the paper listed the following assumption:

the grant proposal assumptions were stated

each assumption was discussed

the assumption was explained by the presenter

there were too many assumptions in the study

HYPOTHESIS

there is some support for the hypothesis

it has been hypothesized that

the hypothesis that there will be

the following hypotheses are postulated

the research hypothesis revealed

the statistical hypothesis makes a statement about

the results supported the hypothesis that

the research findings failed to support the hypothesis

the hypothesis has been identified

the hypothesis was not supported in the research

the hypothesis was formulated by

after reviewing the literature, a hypothesis was formed

the following hypotheses were developed for the study

the following null hypothesis are listed below:

three hypothesis were postulated for the study

the hypothesis could not be rejected by the results of the study

the presenter addressed the hypothesis

each researcher formulated a hypothesis

a research hypothesis was developed

the hypothesis was developed to explain

the study was based on the hypothesis that

the researcher hypothesized about

the research article listed the hypotheses

CHAPTER THREE
QUESTIONS
PROBLEMS
DEFINITION
NEED FOR THE STUDY

QUESTIONS

an important question remains

the question is unanswered

the answer to the question is

an interesting question pertaining to the subject is

another research question asks

the question, then, is

the central question at issue

on one crucial question

another major concern is the question of

the question arises as to

the overriding question is

one way to address the question is

the next question concerns

the crucial question that needs to be answered

the core question used was

a question persisting is

questions have been raised from the previous research

the question is what impact will it have on

here we include questions on

a question to be resolved is

questions arose from this viewpoint

the key question that needs to be answered is

it is hoped that the questions raised

questions addressed in the study include

the question this research study seeks to examine is

the research question was addressed by determining

the questions were grouped into major categories

the questions centers on the idea of

the most important question in the study is

one interesting question addressed

the questions were asked to find out information about

information was gathered from the questions

the researcher acted on the question

additional questions were raised in the study

the advocate had questions about the research

the question was agreed upon by the researchers

the question was developed from input

the basic question asked

the dissertation committee asked questions of the candidate

the question capitalized on

the question was composed of

there was some concern about the research question

the question was constructed from

continual questions arose during the course of the study

the questions were distributed to the research team for review

the question highlighted the research area

the question was impractical to study

the question was to lengthy

questions were proposed for future research

study questions were distributed

an array of questions resulted from

the research group formed questions

questions were developed with the theme

the question puzzled the students

reporters raised questions about the research

PROBLEMS

problems were found with the study

a special problem is

a major problem is how to determine the

another problem is associated with

the problem in the present research is

the problem I have identified

the problem gives rise to concerns about

what is the problem with

to overcome these problems

an unexpected problem arose

some different problems are raised

the problem is complicated by

technical problems arose from

the problem with this line of reasoning is

another problem in understanding this position is

the inherent problem is

the problem to be investigated is

the problem spiraled

the problem studied was submitted to

there were substantial problems with the study

the report summarized the problems

the problem target area was

the problem was terminated by

the problems were monumental

the ultimate problem came

the problem was verified

the researcher confirmed the problem

the researcher validated the problem

the problem was addressed in the research

the researcher wrestled with the problem

an added problem in the study was

the committee adhered the researcher's problem

DEFINITION

definitions of the term differ

the definition reflects

the more precise definition is

the operational definition is

the problem in defining the term is

some accepted definitions are

a working definition was established

a global definition was used

there is a lack of consensus on the definition of

the term is defined as

the definition clearly implies that

by the definition it

it's difficult to define

the term can be defined as

we first have to define the term of

after some agreement on the definition

once the term has been discussed and defined

there are many definitions of the term

the following terms need to be defined

the topic was defined by

no attempt was made to define the term

defining the term is difficult

attempts had been made to define

a list of definitions was developed

the definitions were analyzed

the definition was confusing to some

one can acknowledge the definition by

the active definition is

the researcher had an after thought about the definition

the definition was ambivalent

the researcher articulated the definition

the definition baffled the researchers

the definition was developed from

the definition seemed to hinder the researcher

the definition constrained the research

the breadth of the definition

a checklist of definitions was developed for the study

the definition was put into context

the definition was contrary to other research

the definition was clarified in the report

a working definition was developed in the paper

the definitions referred to

the definition was cumbersome

the essay contained the author's personal definition of

a fairly common definition for

a research definition helped explain

the function of the definition

the definition helped guide the research participants

to insure the terms were defined

the immediate definition of the term was

the definition suggested

the meaning of the definition was hard to interpret

the intricate definition was complex to understand

the definition was justified in the article

it was a lengthy definition

the definition was limited to

the definition was indicated in the manuscript

the definition was miscommunicated to the research participants

a newsletter explained the definition

it was a noteworthy definition

the terms were defined and ordered

the point of the definition was

the program defined the research term

the definition was reprised to

NEED FOR THE STUDY

there is a need for further research and study

a study was conducted to determine the need for

therefore, there is a need to study the issue

the rationale and need for the study is

the need for the study involves

finally, there is a great need for this study

there is a particular need for the study

the researcher determined the need for the study by

there is an abundant need for the study

scholars have indicated a need for the study

there is a need for the study to activate

to advance research there is a need for this study

the need for the study is advocated by researchers

one must concede a need for the study

from the literature review one can see a need for the study

the researchers agree there is a great need for the study

some question the need for the study

apparently, there is a need for the study

it is evident there is a need for the study

the visible need for the study

there is a practical need for the study

one can appreciate the need for the study

some researchers were apprehensive about the need for the study

one could argue the need for the study by

there appears to be a need for the study

the basis for needing the study comes from

research is behind in this area and there is a need for the study

the writer saw a need for the study

the article suggests a need for the study

the calculated need for the study

one could classify the need for the study

the recent change causes a need for the study

limited research shows a need for the study

it can be concluded there is a need for the study

there is common need for further study and research

there is a need for the study to compare ideas

after examining the research it was decided that there was a need for the study

there is a continuous need for the study in this area

to contrast the need for the study

there is a daily need for the study

there was no great need for this study

the researcher's plan showed a need for the study

there was a designated need for the study

one can detail a need for the study

the researcher deviated from the need of the study

the researcher discovered a need for the study

there was a dynamic need for the study

early research shows a need for the study

to educate the public there is a need for the study

to eliminate problems there is a need for the study

to insure a need for the study

this essay shows a need for the study

one could estimate a need for the study by

the need for the study is extensive

the facts indicate a need for the study

the research field shows a need for this type of study

the foundation supports a need for the study

the grant proposes a need for the study

a public hearing voiced a need for the study

the researcher introduced a need for the study

the university saw a need for the study

there is an isolated need for the study

several issues revealed a need for the study

there was a joint need for the study

to keep up with changes there is a need for the study

to upgrade standards there is a need for the study

there is a legitimate need for the study

it doesn't diminish the need for the study

likewise, there is a need for the study

there is a literal need for the study

there is a longitudinal need for the study

the need for the study is mandatory

there was difficulty in convincing others of the need for the study

the measurements indicated a need for the study

the research meeting continued to show a need for the study

the need for the research study is monumental

there is a need for this multistage research study

the need for the study was not justified in the report

once the need for the study is established

the circumstances indicated a need for the study

the paper exhibited a need for the study

the previous research established a need for the study

there is a persistent need for the study

the researchers persuaded the committee to see the need for the study

the need for the study was given high priority

the researcher's agenda showed a need for the study

the researchers responded positively to the need for the study

the practitioner did not agree with the need for the study

the researcher formulated a need for the study by

the pilot study showed a need for further study

the need for the study was pursued

the need for the study was quickly identified

the need for the study ranked high in importance

there was a rapid need for the research study

others reacted to the need for the study

a small grant supported the need for the study

critics were reluctant to see the need for the study

the researcher revised the need for the study to show

others saw the need for the study as rubbish and useless

the committee determined there was no need for the study

the scholar failed to show a substantial need for the study

the team was responsive to the need for the study

a strong need for the study was presented by the researcher

the need for the study entailed

the need for the study section of the paper was poorly written

the need for the study could be expanded to include

the need for the study is valuable to

the need for the study indicated the researcher had vision

there were many weaknesses in showing the need for the study

CHAPTER FOUR
REVIEW OF LITERATURE
DISCUSSION
THEORETICAL FRAMEWORK
ADVANTAGES AND STRENGTHS
LIMITATIONS AND WEAKNESSES

REVIEW OF LITERATURE

the review of literature indicated

the literature review contributes to

the review of literature section will address

the review of research and literature reveals

the intent of the literature review is

the review of literature indicates a need for

a historical review of literature found

the review of literature documents the

the review of literature was short

a discussion of selected literature was provided to

an overview of the literature was given to

the author reviews relevant literature

literature was reviewed from several fields

the review of literature was limited

a review of the literature suggested

the review of literature may be useful

the review of literature facilitated the study

the extensive review of literature

a broad literature review helped to

the review of literature accentuated the study

the comprehensive review of literature found

the review of literature alerted researchers to

the review of literature amplified the study

the review of literature was of great magnitude in the dissertation

the strength of the review of literature came

the review of literature answered several questions

it was apparent from the review of literature

the committee was impressed by the review of literature

the article had a strong literature review

the literature review gave attention to

the review of literature was outdated

the brief review of literature was weak

the researcher made strong claims from the literature review

the continuation of the literature review found

the current review of literature emphasized

the detailed review of literature

one could determine from the literature review that

the review of literature was instrumental in the study

the literature review was easy to understand

the review of literature was informative

the study was enlightened by a strong literature review

strong examples were given in the literature review

it was an excellence literature review

the review of literature was exemplary

the researchers were commended on the literature review

many ideas were expressed in the literature review

the literature review was helpful for understanding the study

the review of literature had a strong foundation

the review of literature was important to

the intention of the review of literature

the literature review was aimed at

an interdisciplinary review of literature showed

a review of literature was in the journal article

the study was easily justified in the literature review

several keywords were identified in the literature review

a wide range of information was in the literature review

the literature review introduced some new research studies

the literature review mentioned some outstanding studies

there were some misgivings about the review

a multitude of studies were in the literature review

several key studies were omitted from the literature review

the review of literature was paramount

the review of literature was pertinent to the research

the literature review emphasized several points

the strong part of the literature review was

the literature review progressed

the review of literature was redundant

the literature review helped re-educate the public

the literature review renewed interest in the study

the literature was re-examined in the review

the review of literature focused on

the review of literature was bias

the literature review was appropriate for the study

the literature review was fitting for the research

there was some uncertainty about the literature review

the literature review was useful to other researchers

one could utilize the literature review for

many variables were discussed in the literature review

there was vision in the literature review

an expansive literature review was included

the literature review was an overview

studies were omitted from the literature review

DISCUSSION

the discussion examines several issues

the discussion examined some reasons for

discussions have taken place

the discussion reflected

as discussed in the article

the following discussion addresses

the discussion outlines the

for the discussion, the important aspects are

at the onset of this discussion

turn now to the discussion of

the author's discussion of the study examines

the discussion suggested

the discussion presents the idea that

the discussion confirms

the discussion pertains to

the discussion was useful for the purpose of

the discussion accomplished several things

the discussion summarizes

the discussion advanced the study by

there was a progression in the discussion

the discussion notified the research field about

the discussion revealed new information

many ideas were communicated in the discussion

the discussion spread to others in the field

there were several warnings indicated in the discussion

there were excellent examples in the discussion

the discussion announced plans to

the discussion was persuasive in nature

the discussion proposed several things

it was a moving discussion

key areas were pointed out in the discussion

the discussion was very opinionated

the discussion prepared the reader for

the discussion provided lots of practical advice

the discussion portion of the paper was shallow

there were several trouble spots in the discussion

one can conclude from the discussion

the discussion was overwhelming

the discussion supported the research presented

the discussion was provoking for some researchers

there were some disturbing aspects of the discussion

the intention of the discussion was

it was a rambling discussion

a thoughtless discussion was presented

the discussion drifted away from its original purpose

the discussion endorsed several things

it was a positive discussion

the discussion was a substantial part of the study

the discussion helped to translate the research into understandable terms

it was an earnest discussion

there was a passionate discussion at the conference

the discussion divulged several new ideas

the discussion portion of the paper was disseminated

it was an agreeable discussion

one might oppose some things in this discussion

the discussion seemed to turn into a debate

the discussion had substance

the discussion raised several questions

there was a major discussion on the issues

the discussion seemed to theorize

the discussion was open to speculation

it was an authentic discussion

the discussion was comprehensive and thorough

it was an exhaustive discussion

the discussion was delayed

the discussion stabilized concerns

the discussion produced

the discussion motivated others

the discussion embarked on new ideas

the research spread after the discussion

there were high expectations about the research discussion

the discussion benefited many researchers

the discussion section of the article began to attack

the discussion criticized others in the field

after a boastful discussion

the discussion seemed endless

the researchers made brave statements in the discussion

the audience responded enthusiastically to the discussion

it was a purposeful discussion

the research discussion was a conglomerate of

THEORETICAL FRAMEWORK

the proposed theoretical framework was

theoretical framework were developed to

the theoretical framework provides a base for

the theoretical framework to be implemented

the theoretical framework gave direction to the study

the authors present a theoretical framework

a development in the theoretical framework is

from a theoretical perspective, the framework is

the initial step in the theoretical framework is

the theoretical framework is based on

the theoretical framework may be useful for

the theoretical framework presented the idea of

the basis for the theoretical framework is

the theoretical framework suggested

the theoretical framework is identified by

the information from the theoretical framework indicates

ADVANTAGES AND STRENGTHS

the research has distinct advantages

a major advantage of the study is

strengths of the study include

one major strength of the study is

strengths of the thesis include

the paper's strength was

the central advantage of the report

the specific strengths of the study were

the advantages of this article over others

the strength in the thesis was indicative of

the strength was characterized in the research by

the particular advantages of this paper

some unique advantages of the article

the strength of the report is distinguished by

the strength can be attributed to

some special advantages of the review

there were many elements of strength in the paper

the strengths were featured

the advantages of the research were clear

the explicit strengths of the paper

the advantages of the paper were classified

the strengths were detailed

the advantages were categorized

the designated advantages in the study

the outstanding strengths were recognized in the study

the strengths were manifest

the strengths of the research were commendable

to summarize the advantages

the advantages of the research prevailed

the predominate strength of the research

the review found several advantages in the research

the strength was evident

the advantages were noted

the advantages were documented in the report

the advantages of the research experiment were

one could testify to the strength of the research

the strengths in the paper encompass

the clear-cut advantages of the study was

an explanation of the advantages of the study follows:

the strengths are presented in the paper

the researcher commented on the strengths of the study

the researcher pointed out the advantages

the advantages were described in the report

a short narrative was used to explain the strengths

the advantages were sketched on a chart

the meticulous advantages were discussed

the researcher elaborated on the advantages

the report detailed the strengths of the study

LIMITATIONS AND WEAKNESSES

the major limitations of the study were

some possible limitations are

limitations to this study include

the limitations that should be included

a major limitation of the data

potential limitations include

another limitation comes from

the study has the following limitations

the research study will be limited by

the study had several weaknesses

the weaknesses were detailed in the report

the weaknesses were discussed point by point

the paper was weak in many areas

the weaknesses were uncovered

the limitations narrowed the study

the weaknesses in the grant were mentioned

several limits were determined in the research

the weakness was recounted in the report

there was an analysis of the weaknesses

it was difficult to explain some of the weaknesses

the limitations of the study were wearisome

the research limitations were burdensome

the limitations were challenging in the research

it was not easy to discuss the weaknesses in the study

the weaknesses were troublesome in the research

it was an uphill challenge for the researchers to deal with the limitations

the weaknesses were mystifying

the limitations hindered the study

the weaknesses complicated the research project

the researcher was perplexed by the limitations

there were many stumbling blocks and weaknesses in the study

the researcher was distressed by the limitations

the weaknesses caused the researcher to struggle

the limitations were discouraging

the frustrations came from the limitations

the weaknesses were observed in the study

some weaknesses were detected

the limitations were exposed in the research

the researcher detected a weakness

the limitations were sighted in the study

the research funding was reduced after the limitations were presented

it was upsetting to discuss the weaknesses

the limitations were annoying

the paper contained some alarming limitations

the weaknesses were startling

the limitations threatened the research funding

the research project was successful despite limitations

the research study was briefly delayed by funding limitations

each limitation was explained

weaknesses were reviewed by a special committee

the limitations caused the study to change direction

a paper was written on the limitations

an article highlighted the weaknesses

the grant proposal had numerous limitations

the research director spotted some weaknesses in

the entire research proposal was weak

the researcher refused to address the limitations

graduate students addressed weaknesses in the study

CHAPTER FIVE
METHODOLOGY
DATA
SAMPLE AND POPULATION
SURVEYS
QUESTIONNAIRES

METHODOLOGY

there are several methodological approaches available

the methodological issues are

the methodology is divided into the following categories

there were some methodological weaknesses in the research

the methodology associated with the study

the methodology was designed to provide

the methodological strengths that characterize the study

the paper describes the methodology for

the methodology was modified to

the methodology used in the investigation

the methodology was described in this section

the methodology was used to examine

there were challenges in the methodology

the methodology was flexible

the methodology undertaken in the study was

there was a strong methodology section

the methodology section was questionable

one could dispute the methodological section

the methodology section was vague

there was disagreement about the methodology

the methodology was ambiguous

the methodology raised some important issues

the researcher reflected on the methodology

reference was made of the methodology

the researcher mentioned the methodology

the researchers concentrated their efforts on the methodology

using conventional methodology

a system was in place to conduct the methodology

the methodology was hampered by

the methodology was preserved by

the schedule for the methodology included

a calendar was developed for the methodology

the investigators reviewed the methodology

several types of methodology were explored

the methodology section took shape

the studies had similar methodology

the methodology was simple to understand

the research methodology was extremely complex

mistakes were unavoidable in the methodology

the methodology was appropriate for the field of study

there was a powerful methodology section

the methodology was reinforced by

the proposed methodology

the methodology was submitted to the committee

the methodology was recapped

the tentative methodology was described in the grant

the paper analyzed the methodology

the core of the research was the methodology

students needed assistance in the methodology section

the proposal was strong in methodology

there were problems in the methodology

the methodology section was incomplete

the methodology was a confusing part of the study

students were unclear about the methodology

DATA

data reviewed that

these data suggest

data were analyzed by

the data were compared with

data were generated using

a data-based study revealed

data related to the issues

the initial step in the data collection

the first step in the data collection process

data in the study were categorized using

the pilot study provided data

the data pool consisted of

the author reviewed data from

one source of data is provided

the data presented demonstrate

the data derived from

preliminary data will be collected

the data were collected as part of

the data from the literature is examined

the primary data analysis was designed to

further analysis of the data is needed

the data presented in the current report

additional data must be generated

the data differ from the findings

the analysis of the data was carried out by

it is difficult to complete data

the data in the study consisted of

the analysis of the date demonstrated

the data were consolidated to describe

the data collection instrument consisted of

overall, the data analysis provided

the data demonstrated

the researchers reviewed all the data

the data sustained the study

the researchers had adequate data

researchers outside of the study questioned the data

the scholars were impressed by the data collection

the researchers concluded that the data

the principals of data collection were presented

the data were presented in a logical process

one could assess the data

some were apprehensive about the data collection

one could rationalize some aspects of the data collection

several assumptions could be made about the data

in evaluating the data

there was some anxiety in collecting the data

the data collection was slow and tedious

there was some uneasiness about the data collection

there were some unreasonable requests in the data collection

the researchers were neglectful of the data

the data collection was meticulous

the data were in jeopardy

the data collection was in a crucial state

the data collection was timely

the researcher was given additional time to collect data

timing was crucial in collecting the data

the researcher was disturbed by the data collection

some unreliable workers helped collect the data

the researchers had misgivings about the data

problems were unexpected in the data collection

the data collection process was incomplete

several steps in the data collection were unperformed

the researchers did not make adequate preparations for the data collection

SAMPLE AND POPULATION

the sample was described by

in identifying the sample of

the trends are a sample of

the sample was comprised of

the sample was drawn from

the sample was composed of

a nationwide, random sample encompassed

a different sample plan was developed

the sample for the study will be selected from

the research was conducted with a random sample

the sample population of the survey was

several populations participated in the study

the sample was selected from the population of

the population for selecting the sample was

the sample selection was developed from the population of

the population was identified by

SURVEYS

the survey was administered to

the surveys were sent to

the initial survey requested the respondents to

each survey consisted of

the response rate of the survey was

a recent survey reported

results of an on-going survey

the survey research method was used

the survey was used to evaluate

the survey can be compared to

the surveys correspond with

the similar survey was developed

the survey can be correlated to

a previously published survey was used

developing the survey was difficult because

the survey method was selected to insure

the surveys allowed participants to respond

the survey was very detailed

the survey had a specialty area

the survey was constructed in a way that allowed

the response rate was very promising from the surveys

the survey was revised

the researcher edited the survey

the survey was pre-tested

the final survey contained

difficult items were deleted from the survey

the researcher proof-read the survey

the survey was rewritten to include

the survey was practical and informative

the survey was expanded to include

a letter accompanied the survey

there were some errors in the survey

the survey contained several mistakes

essentially, the survey was easy to read

the survey was significant in that

the essence of the survey

the essential part of the survey was

the survey originated from

the survey was checked for

after the survey was refined

the survey participants were selected

the survey brought out key items

the survey was representative of

the bias in the survey

the survey was feasible

a unique feature of the survey

a highlight of the survey

the survey emphasized

an important part of the survey was

the surveys were distributed to

researchers recorded the results of the survey

several surveys were used in the study

each survey had a purpose

the researchers questioned the survey

surveys were reviewed by the research team

QUESTIONNAIRES

the questionnaire began with

the questionnaire was designed to obtain information

the questionnaire was divided into sections

the data was collected by questionnaires

the questionnaire was designed in such a way

the questionnaire was confusing for the subjects

the final questionnaire was given to the subjects

a panel of researchers revised the questionnaire

a pamphlet was included with the questionnaire

the questionnaire was developed into a brochure

personal information was obtained from the questionnaires

the underlying theme of the questionnaire was

the questionnaire focused on

the questionnaire was presented to

the questionnaire was very helpful

there were favorable responses about the questionnaire

the crucial part of the questionnaire was

the questionnaire was suitable for the study

the questionnaire was historical in nature

the questionnaire was illogical

the subjects commented that the questionnaire was incorrect

the questionnaire was unscientific

the questionnaire was a barrier to the research project

the questionnaire was important to the study

the grant contained a sample of the questionnaire

the questionnaire insinuated

special interest was developed in the questionnaire

it was impossible to predict the response to the questionnaire

it was a remarkable questionnaire

the questionnaire was inadequate

the questionnaire was improperly distributed

the questionnaire was influenced by

the questionnaires were given intermittently

the questionnaire in the paper was too long

two departments developed a joint questionnaire

the questionnaire was filled with difficult language

a shortcoming of the questionnaire was

the questionnaire was insufficient for the study

a research assistant administered the questionnaire

an important item was omitted from the questionnaire

the questionnaire was arranged to include

the original questionnaire was to brief

the researcher envisioned the questionnaire

it was a resourceful questionnaire

the university committee gave permission to distribute the questionnaire

the questionnaire was workable for the study

the results of the questionnaire were kept confidential

each questionnaire was specifically designed to

graduate students developed questionnaires

a questionnaire was used in the pilot study

the questionnaire was confusing

there were concerns about the questionnaire

questionnaires were lost in the study

CHAPTER SIX
CONCLUSION
FINDINGS
RESULTS

CONCLUSION

the main conclusion is

the author is lead to the following conclusions

several conclusions indicated

other interesting conclusions are

the study fails to support the conclusion

in conclusion, it is recognized

in conclusion, it is evident that there

the interim conclusion is

several general conclusions were reached

another conclusion was found

the study supports the principle conclusions

another conclusion that may be drawn from

in conclusion, a re-examination is needed

in conclusion, the following points were summarized

the conclusion points out

the most significant conclusion of the study

the conclusions were condensed in the published paper

the conclusions were adapted

a powerful conclusion was presented in the article

the conclusions were strong in the paper

a comprehensive conclusion was included

the conclusions were practical

regarding the general conclusions

in reference to the conclusion

the research candidate was asked to rewrite the conclusion section of the paper

the conclusion was very limited

the researcher refused to expand the conclusions

the conclusion portion of the report was confusing

the conclusions were plentiful

the conclusions were sufficient for the study

the conclusions were misrepresented in the paper

the conclusions did not do the study justice

the doctoral committee approved the candidate's conclusions in the study

the conclusions were adapted by the research team

the researchers verified the conclusions by

a special acknowledgment was noted about the conclusion portion of the paper

the conclusions were delivered to the grant funding foundation

the conclusions were unintentionally omitted

the conclusions developed from the grant project benefited

the conclusions section was completed by the team

support for the project was gained from the conclusions

the conclusions were accurate and reliable

the conclusion were realistic

the conclusions were carefully stated

the committee was critical of the conclusions

the conclusions were reasonable

the rationale behind the conclusions

the researcher skillfully presented the conclusions

after a close examination of the conclusions

the conclusion received a nod of approval

the response at the conclusion of the study was positive

there was a negative response to the conclusions

the university endorsed the conclusion in the study

the conclusions were passed on to the participants

the funding source acquired the research conclusions

the conclusions produced lots of interest in the subject

following the conclusions the department was more committed to the study

the conclusions interfered with another study

the ever-changing conclusions

the conclusions addressed several concerns

the conclusions were easily appreciated

the researcher clarified the conclusions

the research committee admired the investigators conclusions

the conclusions were satisfactory for the study

the conclusions were viewed in high regard

lots of praise was given to the researchers conclusions

recognition was given at the conclusion of the study

the conclusions were held in high esteem by the research community the conclusions revealed new areas of research study

the conclusions were communicated to

the conclusions brought to light

the conclusions advanced this important research

the conclusion section provided leverage for future funding

the conclusion set a precedence for the future

this conclusion will greatly influence other research

some researchers resented this conclusion

the journal immediately published the conclusion

the conclusions were circulated to the committee

the conclusions were disseminated to the press

researchers ere surprised by the conclusions

research articles were written about the conclusions

the conclusions were addressed at conferences

FINDINGS

among the findings are

some generalizations can be made from the findings

the study findings indicate

the findings suggest the need for

the findings were surprising

the findings in this study document

the findings were discouraging

a key finding is

the findings seem to suggest

the findings are derived from

the findings were relevant

the findings support the assumption that

the findings raised some questions

the research produced some major findings

the most important finding was

the findings are controversial

the findings provide a basis for

the most significant finding in the project was

the findings have implications for

the most interesting findings in the study is

the article integrates the findings

the final report explains the findings

findings in the study are important to

the findings in the present study do not address

a major finding indicated

the findings show a need for further research

the findings were significant for future research

the significance of the findings appear

the findings have important meaning to

some important questions were raised from the findings

a statement could be made about the findings

the major contributions of the finding

the findings were displayed in a research exhibit

the findings were published abroad

the findings exposed some negative issues

the findings were broadcasted in the region

the findings advanced new techniques

the findings stimulated others

subsequently, the findings revealed

the findings agitated others in the field

the findings were offensive to some people

the researcher was a little upset by the findings

many supported and agreed with the findings

the findings concurred with other studies

the findings were destructive in some ways

there was much agreement on the findings

the researcher came to term with this finding by

the aim of the findings was to

the findings focused in several directions

the findings seemed pointless

the findings seemed to drift

the findings alarmed the conference participants

a warning was given in the findings

the findings were long and extensive

some commented that the findings were weak

the findings were similar to

the findings duplicated another study

a collection of the findings was formed

the findings were quite acceptable to the group

almost all of the findings centered around

the findings served a practical purpose

the findings were translated in several languages

the findings did not replace other studies

the findings are reshaping the thinking of

the findings helped to reconstruct

one finding was important in reforming

the finding altered and modified

an alternate finding emerged

the findings were examined collectively

the findings were dissected

some central features of the findings

the findings infuriated the organization

one could understand the displeasure of the findings

the findings were disclosed

once the findings were released

the findings predicted

the findings were presented in a bulletin

it was decided to publicize the findings

some were disgusted with the findings

the findings of the research projects are presented annually

RESULTS

the results of the study supported

the resulted are relative to the

the results of the research suggested

based on the results it can be stated

the results can be documented

the preliminary results were presented

results have implications for

the results were overwhelming

the results were compared to

the results from the study indicated

no results have been published

the results support the idea of

the results go a long way

the results will help future researchers to

the results were somewhat weak

the results answered many questions

the committee remarked about the results

the researcher answered for the results

no one claimed responsibility for the results

the results were sound and firm

there was a rebuttal in response to the results

the researcher made a written reply about the results

there was hostility about the results

the research community anticipated the results

the outlook for positive results was promising

the researcher couldn't begin to predict the results

many were impatient to find out the results

there was much satisfaction with the research results

the results of the article were argued

the researcher cleared up questions about the results

the results were justified

apparently the results were suspicious

it was evident from the results

the results were difficult to interpret

the results were fascinating

the audience had a favorable impression of the results

the results materialized

the researcher reflected on the results

the results were a break through

the results were utilized

the results were adapted

one could apply the results to

the results of the research were dedicated

the investigator concentrated on the results

the results were minimal

the results did not address

the forthcoming results

the results were upheld

the results were unscientific

the committee praised the results

the results were approximate

there was a battle over the results

a major exchange arose over the results

the results were arranged

the results perplexed the researcher

the researcher articulated the results

the results bewildered the doctoral committee

the students assembled to hear the results

there was some agreement about the results

the results were finally calculated

the results were a collaboration

there was much speculation about the results

the results were astounding

many things were inferred from the results

the results were discussed at length

positive results were attained

attention was given to the results

researchers were preoccupied with the results

the author attacked the results in the article

the results were available and accessible to other researchers

the results were shared

it was important to keep the results confidential

the results were handled poorly

the results were faulty

there were some stumbling blocks in calculating the results

one barrier in determining the results was

the results helped establish a new discipline

in the beginning the results were overlooked

the results were tarnished from

CHAPTER SEVEN
SUMMARY
RECOMMENDATIONS
IMPLICATIONS
COMPUTER RESEARCH PHRASES

SUMMARY

the article summarizes previous research

the summary puts into context the

in summary, the authors have presented

one could summarize that

the summary revealed

to summarize, several explanations were offered

in sum, the paper indicates

in sum, it would appear

in summarizing this explanation

the summary explores

the summary is an effort to

summarizing the report is difficult

in summary, one must note

the previous summary found

the summary has future implications for

the extensive summary opens the doors for

the summary identified

specific changes were part of the summary

the summary was significant

the summary was a long explanation of

the summary marked a turning point

in reference to the summary

several points were addressed in the summary

closing remarks were included in the summary

the author drafted the summary

the summary was vital to the study

a paramount part of the summary was

the summary was a required part of the grant

the researcher summarized the fundamental parts of the study

the summary was compelling

the summary was crucial to future research

the most binding aspect of the summary was

there were several negative aspects in the summary

the summary was inattentive to

contrary to the summary

the summary seemed to contradict the rest of the study

the committee praised the well written summary

the summary was useful for others

the impartial summary

several discoveries were revealed in the summary

the summary was incomprehensible

the summary was complicated and unclear

the summary was objectionable

it was a meaningful summary

the summary was candid and open

the researcher's opinion was expressed in the summary

the summary surmised

some researchers were hostile about the summary in the study

the study summary was argumentative

some researchers were optimistic following the summary

the summary was coordinated with

a program was aligned with the summary

adjustments were made in the summary portion

the summary was distributed by mail

the summary portion of the article was resourceful

discussion was generated from the summary

it was inventive summary

the summary inspired other studies

the summary was original and creative

the researcher had a very orderly summary

the summary will be productive for the future

otherwise, the summary had a few weak points

overall, the summary was excellent

it was an overrated summary

the importance of the summary was overemphasized

the summary of the article had to be shortened

there was some hesitation about the summary

opinions were swayed after the researcher presented the summary

the summary was a strong representation of the research project

a rough draft of the summary was submitted

the scope of the summary

the summary took a path of action

it was a very influential summary

the summary provided feasible

the summary was a tribute to

the research summary served several functions

the summary was both realistic and down-to-earth

it was an intense and powerful summary

the summary yielded positive outcomes

RECOMMENDATIONS

the recommendations are relevant

further research is recommended

a recommendation from the study

recommendations for improvement were made

the researcher recommends

important recommendations were made

the recommendations justify

revised recommendations were made

further study is recommended

there is a recommendation for further investigation

the recommendations need to be considered

these new recommendations have been developed

the recommendations are based on the findings

some new approaches are part of the recommendations

some interesting aspects emerged from the recommendations

the recommendations are profound

the recommendations raised some issues

the recommendations set high standards

the recommendations drifted from the study

there is a recommendation that determines

the recommendations far exceeded the standards

the rationale behind the recommendations was

there was a backlash toward the recommendations

the response mentioned the recommendations

the research group was receptive of the recommendations

there was a tremendous amount of substance to the recommendations

they were broad-minded recommendations

the recommendation was sensible

the recommendations reached far limits

they were wise recommendations

the recommendation was called into question

the recommendations conveyed

the recommendations provided guidance

it was urged in the recommendations

the recommendations helped to document

the plan was reconstructed from the recommendations

the recommendations became part of the record

there were debates over the recommendations

the researcher's testimonial included the recommendations

after the recommendations were published

the recommendations were presented in a scientific research report

the recommendations were listed in the paper

they were descriptive recommendations

the recommendations recaptured the enthusiasm

the committee was satisfied with the recommendations

the recommendations stated that

one could interpret the recommendations

the recommendations accounted for

each recommendation was addressed

the study had positive recommendations

the recommendations were addressed by

each recommendation was discussed

the university administrators examined the recommendations

each researcher made recommendations for

the department chair did not agree with the recommendations

IMPLICATIONS

the implications are fundamental to

several implications are

the implication for researchers is

reference was given to the implications

the implications were connected by

there was a link in the implications

the potential implications are

things were insinuated from the implications

the implications were hard to understand

the implications had hidden meaning

the implications symbolized

the implications were useful in the study

there was a distinction in the implications

the implications were far reaching

the implications were overshadowed by

the paper contained significant implications

not much attention was given to the implications

the implications put emphasis on

the foremost implications

the extensive implications were

a valuable implication was

take note of the implications

despite the influence of the implications

considerable thought went into the implications

one essential implication was

the researcher must determine how the implications

the implications seemed unreal

they were stirring implications

the implications were very idealistic

the researcher elaborated on the implications

the implications need to be expanded

a weakness in the study was the implications section

COMPUTER RESEARCH

the data were computer analyzed for

a computer screen was utilized in the study to

using a computer mouse the subjects were

several advantages of using the computer in the study were

the web site was accessed

the computer generated illustrations were obtained

cut and paste editing was performed on the computer to

the computer was used to create

a computer version appropriate for the study was

the search engine was used to retrieve research information

subjects were randomly selected from the computer address book

an e-mail was sent to prospective subjects

the researcher browsed the web for information to

research information came from several internet sources

the research was discussed in a computer chat session

the research was collaborated on an e-mail bulletin board

the computer chat session located other researchers to distribute the research

the research information was downloaded

numerous web sites were utilized for the study

research topics were organized on the computer

research files were uploaded to a directory

the home page provided useful information for the researcher by

the home page presented a menu of research topics

the literature was downloaded to the documents folder

file archives were used to access the research tape

the topic was researched through the database

the directory of servers was used in researching the subject

the computer modem connected the

newsgroups were used to research articles

the internet was used to obtain a broad level of information

computer monitors were used to observe

client programs were developed to answer research questions

for security the research file was copied and stored in

many internet resources were implemented in the study

the subjects in the study communicated by e-mail

questionnaires were returned through the system mailbox

the on-line server was used to access the internet

a directory name was given to each area of research

mail lists were used to establish research discussion groups

responses to the research were left on the local bulletin board

news readers were used to sort the article in the study

research information was stored in a compressed file

a program to prevent viruses was installed in the hard drive

bookmarks of web sites were created for this research study

keywords were developed for the literature search

the world wide web was used for the study

the researcher browsed the world wide web for information

new folders were created to categorize the research files

research web locations were placed on the computer map

computer hardware was purchased for the study

a variety of computer software programs helped store the research information

the research material was presented by computerized tables

the research folders were color-coded on the computer

after the pilot study a new research document was created

graphic computerized images were recorded in a scanner

an address book was developed to list the research participants

research responses were saved on the computer for future study

computer printouts were generated for the study

software programs were reviewed in the study

research responses were viewed on-screen

information on prospective subjects was gathered through a computer network

research information on the organizations was obtained from a computer listing

nation wide information on the subjects was accessed through the computer

students accessed the research information on personal computers

a computerized information network provided the researcher with

e-mail was used to save time by reaching numerous addresses

research files were downloaded to received information

the weakness of this computer software was

the research message were posted on computer message boards

up-to-date information was obtained from the internet

the researcher surfed the world wide web for random web sites

user names were used for identifying the researchers

important research articles were flagged on the computer list

new files were added as the research expanded

on-line information was used to access multiple research results

a new program was installed after the old files were discarded in the trash

statistical studies were performed with a computer calculator

graphs of the research were stored in the scrap book

the computer word dictionary was used to check spellings and terms in the study

the sound data was stored on a CD

the printer produced a sharp image of the computer graph

the electronic mail in the research study was slowed due to high traffic

the laser printer produced high quality graphics for the study

a user group was formed to share research information

through computers the research was conducted faster and more efficiently

problems with the printer delayed the study

research information was lost on a corrupted disc

a limitation of the study came from the small hard drive storage

the research text and questions were computer generated

the date and time of the research was documented on a computer

research mailing labels were generated on a computer

computer graphics were an important part of the research study

electronic discussions were used in the study

electronic journals helped in obtaining research information

the information was downloaded from college computer to personal computer

the internet was a key source in conducting the research

the resources for the research project were obtained from the internet

on-line communication helped the researchers exchange information

an article was posted in a news group to obtain research information

on-line library catalogs were used to review records

research documents were obtained through internet sources

the researchers were connected through an internet link network

the bibliographic research was found through internet library catalogs

each researcher had a laptop computer

computer terminals were used as part of the study

the subjects answered survey questions on a computer

graduate students researched information on the internet

research results were obtained quickly with computers

computer problems slowed the research

the lack of computers made the research project difficult

researchers were trained in new computer techniques

the research was conducted entirely on a computer

confidentiality was an issue for research conducted on computers

computer security measures were used in the research study

problems with the computer were addressed in the research article

the article was generated on a computer

grant proposals were submitted on computer disks

electronic submissions of the research papers were encouraged

the final research report was submitted on a computer disk

ABOUT THE AUTHOR

Susan Louise Peterson is a native of Oklahoma and has worked professionally as a college professor and public school teacher. She has a Ph.D. in Family Relations and Child Development from Oklahoma State University and a Masters degree in Human Relations from the University of Oklahoma. Her Undergraduate study was in the area of Sociology at the University of Science and Arts of Oklahoma. Over the past years, Susan has written articles for professional journals, composed book reviews, presented papers at academic conferences, and has been involved in grant proposal development. As a college professor, Susan enjoyed endless hours of reading and revising term papers.